Dedication

This book is dedicated to my daughter, Sasha, who has helped me be a better human and grow in ways I never knew I should. She is a brilliant light who amazes people everywhere she goes. Not because of her gender identity but because of her humanity, empathy and passion – words I never imagined using to describe my daughter but now as though custom made for her. I love you with all my heart and then some.

And to my son, Michael, who constantly inspires me by his fervent expressiveness and enveloping whole-hearted hugs. I love looking at the world through his lens, as though it's the very first time. I love you so much.

My world is far better with you both in it.

Acknowledgements

Thank you to Brian Swanson who started this journey by a simple introduction to a phenomenal human, my publisher, agent, friend, Ken Rochon Jr. And thank you to Michelle Mras for mentoring me. Michael Mras, the genius editor, I thank you! So many thanks to the wind beneath my wing-ers ~ Renee Maisel, Lisa Czelatdko, Claudine Dickson, Megan Bollman, Rodney Gullatte, Emily Sherwood, Suzanne Tulien, Julie Miller Davis, Debbie Swanson, Monique Lewis, Misty Stuart, Kathi Wickizer, Caryn Adams, Dr, Lynn Vidler, Susan Saksa, Regina Romrell, Fabrizio Labate, Elizabeth Egnaczyk, Katie Pace, Tina Dewey ~ thank you for the encouragement, perspectives, the inspo and the many, many drinks! I love you all!! Thank you to Krys & Kiersten Fakir for bringing my vision to reality with the back cover art. And last but certainly not least, thank you to Ron Voss for being supportive in countless ways to help this book come to fruition. I love you and I could not have asked for a more incredible dad to parent our beloved Sasha and Michael.

Foreword

"You never get a second chance to make
a first impression."
~ *Oscar Wilde*

First impressions are made within seconds between people. Once a first impression is made, all the other impressions are either reinforcing or rebuking the first. When a life is concerned, first impressions and first responses are critical. When I was asked by Kat Voss to write an introduction for her book, The First 10 Seconds, I immediately agreed.

I heard about the topic of her book months prior. I was intrigued for two reasons: First, I had not heard of a book on this topic. Second, I have both witnessed first-hand and heard second-had the ramifications when those crucial 10 Seconds are handled poorly.

10 Seconds are a mere fraction of a minute, yet they can build or break a lifelong relationship with a child, friend, parent, sibling, partner or co-worker. When we are entrusted with the essence of another, this information needs to be received in the most open and accepting manner. There is a methodology explained within the pages of this book.

Get out of your head. This is not about you. It is about that person who trusts you emphatically. Stop. Be Present. Love. Support. Because in the end, the decision is theirs. You can choose to be a part of their support system or abandon the one who trusted you.

"There are three types of business: Mine, Yours and God's" ~ Byron Katie

There are times when wisdom comes along to help you navigate through a difficult period of your life. Perhaps, this book you are holding is the wisdom you seek. Whether you are reading this to support a loved one, or you are wondering how to come out to someone you love, The First 10 Seconds are crucial, don't squander them. Just like first impressions, you can not have another first reaction.

– Dr. Michelle Mras

Dr. Michelle Mras is an award-winning, internationally recognized inspirational speaker, published #1 Best Selling Author, intuitive leader, wife, and mother who has been stirring audiences and individuals to action through her compelling message of self-leadership, resilience, and living a life of intention. Michelle's infectious presentations and coaching inspire her clients to rise above negative self-talk to reclaim their inner grit.

Michelle encourages you to be your best version every day and live unapologetically. Her fiery spirit and passion drive her to candidly share the key moments that transformed her into the irresistible force she is today. MichelleMras.com

Chapter 1

"Love begins with an acceptance of the person as they are. Our primary focus is on loving the person, come what may. Part of love is helping them become the best they can be."
~ *Donna Goddard, Touched by Love*

I'm glad you're here! Now let's talk about why. Some readers are transgender and read everything they can find on the subject. Another group might be part of a transgender person's comfort network and looking for all the best ways to be supportive. Perhaps someone gave you this book. Maybe they said, "Hey, [Mom, Dad, Partner, Sibling, Friend, Boss…] I have a book I'd like for you to read."

If you're with the latter group, then chances are that someone in your life is transgender. You might even be asking yourself, "What is transgender anyway?" Transgender is a term used to describe a person whose sense of personal identity and gender does not correspond to the sex they were born with. You might not have even discussed it with them before. Quite possibly, they have given you this book to help you prepare for an important conversation that they would like to have with you soon.

The thing about these types of conversations is that just like so much of parenting, there is no manual to prepare you to hear and react to the enormous weight of these words from your loved one. I've talked to families who say they kind of always knew or suspected that someone close to them was gay or bi or trans. I've heard stories where the young person said that they needed to talk to their family about something important and the parent said, "Is this about you being gay?" Those conversations are often a great deal easier, I imagine, because there has been time to process. Some families have told me that they have never had a "coming out" conversation because it was always understood, supported and a complete nonissue. No elephant in that room!

But for some of us – and yes, I mean me – one day a young son sits down to tell his mother that he's transgender. The mother in this scenario is indeed shocked but not at all negatively surprised. I never suspected that either of my children were anything besides the phenomenal humans I gave birth to many years before. Immediately I said, "Ok, I know what I think transgender means. So tell me what it means to you so we're on the same page!" (We were on the same page but I've definitely deepened and broadened my understanding from that initial conversation.)

My children are both adults and have not lived at home for many years although I've always stayed in close communication. They've developed their own rhythms in life and it's been interesting, exciting, heartwarming, humbling, intimidating and sometimes worrisome to see them both make their way forward and succeed in their young adult lives. The one constant in their lives in regard to their family relationships is that they know with absolute certainty that their parents adore and love them more than anything in the world. So the thought of "Where do we go from here?" was all about navigating forward together.

When I began this journey with my new daughter, I did a lot of research on the subject. I wanted information on everything involving the subject of transgender. The most startling numbers available and mentioned in nearly every article are the very high statistics for suicide. I felt compelled to do something about this. So I started writing a version of what you're reading now.

I believe that when something huge is revealed to a person, it's what happens in those first 10 seconds (your initial reaction) that will always be remembered. If the reaction is negative, no matter how many times you apologize, it will always be the memory of that moment.

I write and share these words in hopes that you will find the reasons you need, from wherever you stand on morals, values and beliefs, to positively recognize this person in your life as they journey on toward self-development, acceptance and empowerment. My goal is to help you make those first 10 seconds of this revelation conversation into something that will always be remembered for good reason.

Chapter 2

"Four things you can't recover: The stone after the throw, the word after it's said, the occasion after it's missed, and the time after it's gone."
~ *Deanna Wadsworth*

It's important to find reasons to support someone who is transgender. And by support, I mean, respecting and loving them, whether your values, beliefs or morals align with them.

If you're reading this book, then chances are someone in your life whom you love or care about is possibly transgender. Let's talk about facts first. (Chapter 6 is a more complete glossary of terms if you find you are unsure about a particular definition.)

Here are some basic facts[i,ii,iii]:

1. LGBTQ+ stands for Lesbian, Gay, Bisexual, Transgender, Queer and others. (Described and defined in Chapter 6.)

2. Gender Identity is a person's sense of self, being male or female or sometimes not being able to neatly name the gender they believe they are.

3. Transgender is defined as a person whose gender identity does not align with their birth sex.

4. Transition is the act of aligning a person's mental, emotional, physical and spiritual being to their gender identity.

5. Non-binary is a person whose gender identity does not fit either male or female genders. Binary means two of something and this person's sense of self is defined outside of the two main genders.

6. A trans man is a person who was born female but transitions to male.

7. A trans woman is a person who was born male but transitions to female.

8. Gender expression is the way a person expresses their gender identity, often through the way they dress, the pitch of their voice and their behavior.

9. Sexual Orientation describes a person's perpetual standard of romantic and sexual attraction. This could be to someone of the opposite sex, same sex or even to both sexes. Simply put, it is determined by the gender of the person(s) to whom they're attracted.

10. As of 2022, approximately 1.4 million people aged 13 and over identify as transgender in the US.

11. California, Georgia, Hawaii, New Mexico, Vermont, Mississippi, Oklahoma, Oregon, Florida and Delaware have the highest population of transgender residents as of 2022.

12. US Transgender women make up 25.5% of the transgender population. Transgender men make up 38.5% of the transgender population and just under 36% identify as nonconforming to either specific gender.

13. In 2021, there were 57 transgender people murdered in the United States. In 2020, 44 murders were committed against members of the transgender community. Many of those cases involved anti-transgender bias. In other cases, their gender identity put them at risk and they were forced into unemployment, poverty, homelessness and/or survival sex work. These cases also validate the claim that Black transgender women are at highest risk. This growing epidemic has pushed lawmakers to expand hate crime laws and, in some cases, institute them.

14. The Trevor Project is the world's largest suicide prevention and mental health organization for LGBTQ young people. The Trevor Project surveyed almost 34,000 LGBTQ youth in 2022, with 48% identifying as transgender. (There is less hard data broken out for Transgender/ Non-Binary Only in this report. It is provided where the report had it available.) Their findings[iv]:

    a. 45% of these surveyed LGBTQ youth seriously considered attempting suicide in 2021.

b. The youth that believed they had good support from their families attempted suicide less than half the rate of those without that familial support. Thirty-two percent of those transgender youth identified their homes as supportive.

c. One in five transgender/non-binary youth attempted suicide in 2021.

d. LGBTQ youth who believed they had LGBTQ support in their schools reported lower rates of suicides than those without school support. 51% of those Transgender/Non-Binary youth identified their school as supportive.

e. 60% of LGBTQ youth who requested mental health care in 2021 were not able to get it.

f. 50% of LGBTQ youth between the ages of 13-17 considered suicide in 2021.

g. 18% of LGBTQ youth between the ages of 13-17 attempted suicide in 2021.

h. 37% of LGBTQ young adults between the ages of 18-24 considered suicide in 2021.

i. 8% of LGBTQ young adults between the ages of 18-24 attempted suicide in 2021.

j. The Trevor Project 2022 survey report states, "LGBTQ youth are not inherently prone to suicide risk because of their gender identity or sexual orientation but rather placed at higher risk because of how they are mistreated and stigmatized in society."

As a mother with a child who happens to be transgender, I know I am not alone when I say I would do anything in the world for my child. Especially when I look at the numbers showing such increased rates of suicide when the trans person does not feel supported, I am even more committed to giving my child what she needs by way of love, respect, care and concern.

At the beginning of this chapter, I wrote, "It's important to find reasons to support someone who is transgender. And by support, I mean, respecting and loving them, whether your values, beliefs or morals align with them." If your values, beliefs or morals don't align with your child, how can you make peace with this vastly different lifestyle from the one you might live or might have expected your child to live? For me, my bottom line is that this is my child. I personally am not hung up on who they love or what they want to be called. This is my child. Whether your child is young and still dependent upon you or grown and just wants to be honest and ask for your support, we're still talking about your child. It is possible to put our own fears and judgments to the side in an effort to let our children know that they are loved no matter what. I never expected to parent my children like my own parents did with me. I just hoped that I would maybe do a little bit better. If each generation does a little bit better parenting than the one before, then this world is evolving with promise!

Chapter 3

"Every story has an end. But in life, every
ending is just a new beginning."
~ Anonymous

Sasha's Story

On February 2, 1987, I gave birth to the most perfectly healthy, beautiful baby boy, Ryan Christopher. My sweet boy was adorable and I loved holding him every single second. I was lucky enough to be able to stay home with my new baby every day. Everything about him was so tiny and perfect that I could just watch him sleep or eat or do anything and I was completely amazed. Babies are miraculous and my baby was no exception. He did all of the things that new babies do…he nursed, he learned to eat solid food, he slept like an angel, he started to make sounds that became little words. He laughed and cried and recognized his mama and daddy. He began to crawl and then pull himself up until he started taking his first steps.

When my baby boy was 14½ months old, we welcomed his younger brother. When Michael came along, he was such a good sleeper! This gave me lots of time to continue enjoying Ryan's firsts. He was doing all the toddler activities and since I'd never had a toddler before, I was completely enamored with every single stage. Ryan liked to be held and once he started saying words, he would lift his arms up and say, "Hold you! Hold you!" I remember one time when both babies were fussy, I put Ryan in the baby backpack and infant Michael in the front snuggly while I vacuumed. Everyone except me snoozed away. It was such a wonderful time in life…when I was able to make them perfectly content.

Their dad was a huge help and did everything for them besides breastfeeding. The babies loved their daddy. I remember a million times looking into Ryan 's eyes and wondering what this little person was going to grow up and become. I knew in my heart that he would be an amazing person who would do big things.

As Ryan got older and bigger, he still amazed me but nothing stood out about him that made me think there was anything amiss about him. While in his teens, he was diagnosed with a high functioning form of Autism ~ Asperger's Syndrome. It was clear that Ryan was quiet but he didn't connect to other people in the same way that his brother did. I didn't worry about it at the time. I remember thinking that maybe he was just more reserved and introverted like his dad.

When he graduated from high school, I made a scrapbook album about his life from birth to 18 years. I noticed that at 7 or 8 years old, he stopped smiling in pictures, whether they were school pictures, family pictures and even most candid photos. He was so silly when he was younger but then he got more serious. I never noticed it until I was putting his photos into the scrapbook. That's significant now but at the time, I didn't think anything about it. I just thought he was a more serious person and he was growing up and maturing.

He excelled in everything he wanted to do. His grades were outstanding. Ryan joined Civil Air Patrol in high school. He struggled with some of the social aspects of it but he did so well with the physical and mental parts that he was assigned to be Commander of his CAP unit. When Ryan graduated from high school, he decided to join the Air Force Reserves. We thought this would be a great career move because he did so well in the structure of Civil Air Patrol.

By the time that Ryan was 26 years old, he owned his own house, and led a very responsible life. His dad and I checked in on him regularly and there were issues where we helped by giving him direction. But overall, he did very well. After staying in the Air Force Reserves for six years, he left the military and was hired by a government contractor company doing pretty much the same job but for even more money. He spent his career on his computer and he also made friends playing computer games in his off time. I was happy to see him making connections with other people, even if it was rooted in computer gaming.

When he was in his mid-twenties, I had started running and entering races. Ryan and I ran several together. He flew out to one of my races to see me cross the finish line of my first half marathon. We often ran one of a local bar's weekly runs. I had many running buddies and we'd run all together and then have a beer or dinner afterwards.

At this point, Ryan had a great job and was making lots of money and seemed fairly content with life. He didn't venture out a lot unless it was with me or his dad and he still played lots of video games but again, I thought this was just how Ryan was and he seemed happy to me (as happy as Ryan ever got!)

One afternoon, Ryan texted me and asked if we could have dinner, just the two of us, because he wanted to talk to me about something. Ryan came over, we ran together then had dinner. I asked him what was up and he said that he'd like to talk to me once we got to my house. As a mom, you have this sixth sense and mine was a foreboding feeling. Something was wrong and I was quite concerned but we had a good conversation over dinner then got to my house. He sat down in the living room and I sat down across from him.

At this point, Ryan's dad and I had gotten divorced but were still close. The day that I moved out of the house the year before, Ryan stopped talking to me completely. He didn't return any texts or calls. We were talking a lot before I moved out. He and his brother knew what was going on so I was really surprised. I continued to text and leave voicemail messages so he knew that I loved him. Five and a half months later, he was coming to his brother's show and I was as well. I stood inside the door waiting to see him but not sure how he would react. He walked in, walked straight up to me and gave me a hug like no other. Everything was wonderful and we didn't talk about what happened. We just moved on.

So on this night when Ryan came to my house and sat down in my living room, he started the conversation with…

"You know when I stopped talking to you after you moved out of the house? Well, I knew you had lots of support and Dad didn't have very much. I didn't feel like I could be supportive of you both while I was going through some of my own stuff. Mom, I'm transgender." And there it was.

Immediately I said, "Well, I know what I think transgender means. Can you tell me what it means to you so we're on the same page?" Ryan explained his highly intellectual definition and we were definitely on the same page. I said, "Great!! Where do we go from here?"

Sometimes I'm quick and sometimes I trip over my own tongue but in those first ten seconds, I reacted from the hip and the heart. There isn't anything I can imagine that I wouldn't support with my children involved. We had some great discussions that evening. He had started the hormone therapy just three months prior to our conversation. He said that he told some of his friends about it already and was very supported. I was the first family member to hear about it. A week or so later, he told his dad and that went very well. Then he told his brother, Michael, which went smoothly, as expected. Not long after that, he called his grandmother. With her experience teaching social work classes, she was completely accepting. Ryan made it clear to everyone that we were not expected to use different pronouns at that point but he would let us all know when that time came.

Then Ryan did something extremely wise. He started stockpiling his money to save for the surgeries that he wanted for the feminization process. He sold his house for a nice profit. He moved out of state to be with his friends ~ the ones who knew and were so supportive. Once he moved away, he legally changed his name to Sasha and then asked for us to start using she/her pronouns.

Sasha's dad and I struggled for several years to not call her Ryan or use the wrong pronoun. I know that she wasn't happy when we messed up. I had to remind her occasionally that I had been calling her Ryan since well before she could talk. I'm sure those years were difficult at times for her and I felt awful when I made a mistake. She wanted so badly to know that she looked appropriate as a female but when we misused pronouns, it felt to her like she didn't appear female enough.

Sasha had grown her hair out so it was very long. She's my tall and slender kid so her hands and features were proportionate to a girl who was on the taller side. She found doctors who specialized in transgender surgeries and was fortunate to be able to afford them. Because she had saved up so much money, she was able to take time away from working for about two and a half years. Once she was ready to go back to work, she found a wonderful job doing what she was doing before but this time with her new legal name.

This journey with my girl has been so fun, unique, and heartwarming. I love when we do mom and daughter days together. She is very feminine looking but dresses in a more androgenous style. Certainly she is still the little person I birthed all those years ago but she IS different and I'm so proud to explain how.

Once Sasha transitioned, I chose to call her Sasha even when I'm talking about her as an infant. So when Sasha was little, she would kiss and hug like any little kid. But as she got older and more serious, her affections stopped. She became very intellectual, always factual and devoid of tenderness and most emotion. She gave the obligatory hugs but they were quite sterile.

When Sasha began transitioning, I saw a very different person. It was subtle but she would hug more. She would say, "I love you" first before I said it when we signed off on our phone calls. She became more affectionate. I was constantly floored by this new side of her. We didn't really talk about it but I soon came to realize that as she became more at home with the physical changes, she became more comfortable in her own skin. This past year, I got to spend some time with her and her life partner. It was so sweet to see her reach over and affectionately rub her partner's back. In some ways, I've been waiting for this version of my child for a long time. I just didn't realize that it had everything to do with becoming who she was supposed to be.

In those years when she wasn't affectionate or very emotional, I learned it was because she figured things out. She was unhappy being a boy because it didn't feel right. She wasn't comfortable making friends for a long time because she wasn't comfortable being in a boy's body with all of the male forms of expression. When we have talked about her as a youngster, she is very clear and articulates perfectly, "Mom, I didn't want to BE a girl. I thought I WAS a girl." Suddenly it's a lot easier to understand why she stayed away from people and didn't get emotional and affectionate. She wasn't really allowing herself to live and experience life like everyone else because of the disconnect between her birth gender and her gender identity. That must have been so painful.

I'm so grateful for this journey. I have no doubt that my girl is her true self now. She is happy, excited, warm, thoughtful, affectionate but still intellectual and still loves computer games. She is not mentally ill. She does not have a disorder. She does not have Asperger's Syndrome. I love this 2.0 version of my daughter. Mostly, I love this version because I think she finally loves herself and it's like she found her way home. I wouldn't trade this journey. I'm honored to get to be her mom and venture forward together. She makes me proud every single day. So if you're reading this and you don't know if you can handle doing "the whole transgender thing," as others have said, imagine your child being the best and happiest version of themselves. Now do you really want to deny that? I encourage you to take this journey with your child. There comes a time when it doesn't matter what other people think or what your expectations of life were. I used to say that watching my children's dreams come true was better than seeing my own. Then I realized that watching my children's dreams come true IS my dream! Her dreams so far have come true and she's living proof of the inner and outer beauty that self-acceptance and the affirmation from those around her can help to manifest.

Chapter 4

"Myths are a waste of time.
They prevent progression."
~ Barbra Streisand

The internet is filled with inaccurate information about a lot of topics. I've listed some below that are typical objections to supporting the Trans or LGBTQ+ community.[v]

1. MYTH: Transgender people are just trying to trick society.

   a. FACT: Gender identity is a personal identification as a man, woman, or another label that is less specific. Gender expression are the attributes and social conduct that identify either masculine or feminine or a mix or neither.

   b. As an example of why "tricking society" is not correct, imagine offering a huge pot of money to people to transition to the opposite sex. When this exercise has been played out in workshops, most people will turn down the money for this one reason: "It wouldn't feel right." So imagine if you were born a gender that never felt right. Recognition of the transgender rights movement acknowledges and supports those who truly feel they were born into the wrong birth sex.

    c. This myth continues to encourage the stigma of people who are just confused or purposely trying to mislead society.

2. MYTH: There are only two genders – male and female.

    a. FACT: Most people are cisgender, which is identifying with your birth sex. Science defines gender as male, female and intersex (a person born with a combination of male and female biological features). Because people's identities are often tied into how they fit into the world, being bound into a gender role that doesn't feel right, can have grim consequences.

3. MYTH: Transgender people are just perverts who want to use the bathrooms of the opposite sex. Peeping, assaults and more serious crimes are just begging to happen.

    a. FACT: According to a report from FreedomForAll-Americans.com, 21 states have public accommodations for trans people using public restrooms of the gender to which they identify. In those states with nondiscrimination protection laws, public safety incidents have stayed level; not increased.

4. MYTH: Transgender people are considered mentally ill.

    a. FACT: The definition of a mental disorder is a psychological state that causes significant distress and disability. The American Medical Association and American Psychiatric Association both agree that being transgender is not a mental illness. They have labeled some trans people with Gender Dysphoria which is when someone suffers mental distress because of the conflict between who they believe they are and the gender they were assigned at birth. When struggling with Gender Dysphoria, it can lead to anxiety, depression and suicidal ideation.

    b. When someone is transgender, they might go the route of hormone therapy and other gender affirming surgeries. These are in part, treatment for Gender Dysphoria. Some trans people severely struggle with this and others do not. Some do not surgically transition but simply change their outward appearance by dressing differently and changing the tone of their voice. Inwardly, they feel that they are already that person so it's just the outward features they care to revise. And often that is dictated by economics as well.

    c. When my own daughter was transitioning, I mentioned that once she finished surgeries that she would be able to find someone to love her with the body she was supposed to have. Her response made me rethink everything. "Mom, I'm not doing this to find someone. I may never find someone. I'm doing this to be the person I was supposed to be." And just like that, my heart grew three sizes. Sometimes our kids are so smart and insightful.

5. MYTH: Transitioning is as simple as getting an operation.

    a. FACT: There are so many moving pieces to transition. Medical procedures and hormone therapy are only one facet of changing genders. And not everyone chooses to medically transition. Some trans people will do the legal requirements to change their driver's license and the legal name on their social security number. The Transequality.com website offers help with specific state information.

    b. There are many social changes involved as well. Some will choose to tell a few people in their lives about this change. And even with this small base of people they choose to tell, they don't always get the support they want and need. In that situation, they may choose to keep to themselves and not socialize with others to avoid the pain of judgment. Others want EVERYONE to know and support them. Even when living their lives openly for everyone around to see and know what they are doing, there is potential rejection, judgment and humiliation.

6. MYTH: These people are just confused or looking for attention. They transition and then change their minds so why should I even support them on something when they're going to regret it?

a. FACT: A study conducted earlier in 2022 showed that 97% of transgender people are happy with their decision. That does mean that 3% of the trans population have some regret for transitioning. Some of those will reverse the transition medically and some will not.

b. I don't want to oversimplify this but I have friends who have been married multiple times. But because they are my friends, I support them, change their names in my databases, adjust to using their new name and change them again once they decide to move on. I have also been sitting in the chapel watching the ceremony and knowing with all my heart and soul that, "this isn't gonna last." And sometimes it does. It's not about what might happen down the road. It's about what the trans person asks of you now.

c. There are requirements before beginning hormone therapy that take months to complete, to include assessments by mental health professionals. This is not a process that a trans person can decide one day to begin and the next day is surgery or they start medication.

7. MYTH: Transgender people are just drag queens or cross-dressers.

a. Trans women are less likely to be either of those. Drag queens are typically gay men (although some are hetero) who dress like women for entertainment reasons. For transgender people, they are identifying with a gender and expressing that by the way they dress, the sound of their voice or however they choose to convey their gender. I've never spoken with a trans person who chose to be transgender for the purpose of entertaining other people.

There are many myths that are frankly too ridiculous to cover. I encourage you to Google some of your concerns to find answers. This is also why it is important to sign up for newsletters and workshops to help you better understand the LGBTQ community.

Chapter 5

"I can't promise to fix all your problems,
but I can promise you won't have to face
them all alone."
~ Oscar Oviedo Jr.

How can you prepare for the coming out conversation? If you are the loved one, reading this book will help so you're halfway there!

If you are the transgender person, here are some tips to initiating that conversation[vi,vii]:

1. Prepare yourself for opening or starting the conversation. Practice in a mirror. If possible, practice with a friend who is already supportive.

2. Have a goal in mind for the outcome you would like to see by the end of the conversation. Some examples are below.

    a. "I want my family to hug me and assure me that they all love me no matter what!"

b. "I want my family to still be speaking to me when the conversation is over."

c. "I would like to see everyone stay in the conversation and not storm off."

d. "I want to feel internally peaceful that I got this big step over with because I was honest and authentic with them."

3. Start by telling one person that you believe will be supportive. Maybe having that person sit near you or at least be part of the conversation would help you feel empowered to talk about this.

4. Set the tone for the conversation. Believe in a positive outcome. If you believe the conversation will go badly, it probably will; so be positive.

5. Before you start, close your eyes and take some deep breaths in and out. Focus on love and respect.

6. Acknowledge that the reason you are nervous or anxious is because you deeply care for the person you're going to talk with. If this person isn't someone you care about, you probably aren't that concerned with how the conversation is going to go.

7. Practice empowering affirmations with or around your deep breathing. Some examples are listed below.

a. "I want the conversation to remain respectful."

b. "I am proud of the person I am and who I am becoming."

c. "I have a valuable message and I deserve to be heard."

8. Tell this person that you need to talk to them about something important and you would appreciate it if they could really listen to you.

9. Be direct – "I am transgender. That means …"

10. Talk about how you feel about this, how long you've known, why it's important to tell them. Don't feel pressured to give information that you are not ready or willing to share.

11. Ask this person how they feel about what they've heard. Ask if they ever suspected or if they've ever known anyone else who is transgender. Asking questions like these will show you where this person stands on your carefully planned announcement.

12. If necessary, use a paraphrasing technique. If they make comments or have questions, repeat in your own words what you hear them saying. "So from what I hear, you believe that transgender people are…" It clarifies what you think they're saying but also allows them to correct themselves if your takeaway isn't what they meant.

13. Be prepared with information if they should ask, "How can we support you?" or "What pronouns should we use and when do you want us to start using them?"

14. Regardless of how the conversation ends, assure them that you love them and appreciate them taking the time to listen to you.

15. If the conversation goes well, celebrate! Keep in mind that many people need time to process information and after thinking it through, they may come back and give you the hugs and assurances of love and support.

    If this doesn't go well, reach out to someone. You are not alone. The Transgender Hotline is (877) 565-8860 and it is a transgender-led organization that connects trans people to the community, support and resources they need to survive and thrive.[viii]

Chapter 6

"Change is the end result of all true learning."
~ Leo Buscaglia

Do you remember the woman who announced a death in her family and signed off "LOL" because she thought it meant "Lots of Love?" I wouldn't want you to make a mistake like that so this chapter is filled with some of the basic LGBTQ terms and definitions, along with the LGBTQ flags and explanations. Some of these terms have been discussed in previous chapters.[ix]

LGBTQ: Lesbian, Gay, Bisexual, Transgender, Queer

It can be confusing at times to remember the order of these letters. I always remember that the first two letters (almost) spell "leg."

GENDER IDENTITY: The description of a person's concept of self as male, female or a blend of both or neither, regardless of their birth sex.

GENDER EXPRESSION: This is the term used to describe how a person chooses to express their identity through clothes, make-up, name, pronouns, hair styles, and behavior.

SEXUAL ORIENTATION: This describes a person's gender choice for romantic or sexual partners.

INTERSEX: A gender description of a person born with reproductive organs belonging to both the male and female gender.

GAY: A term used to describe a person who is attracted romantically and sexually to people of their same gender.

LESBIAN: A woman who is attracted romantically and sexually to women.

TRANS: This is the shortened version of the word "transgender."

TRANSITION: This is defined as the process of bringing a person's body or outward appearance into alignment with their gender identity. There are several types of transition.

- **Medical transition** is when the choice is made to use hormone replacement therapy or surgical procedures.

- **Legal transition** is the process of legally changing one's name and acquiring new documents such as driver's license, passport, bank records, social security information, etc.

- **Social transition** is the process of telling people close to you about your new steps, asking them to call you a different name and pronouns, and dressing and grooming differently.

TRANSGENDER MAN: This describes a person who was born female but has transitioned to be a male.

TRANSGENDER WOMAN: This is a person born male but transitioned to be female.

NON-BINARY: This is a person who identifies outside of male or female genders. Can also be referred to as agender, bigender, demigender or pangender.

PANSEXUAL: This term is used for a person who is attracted to or falls in love with someone regardless of that person's gender.

ASEXUAL: Someone absent of sexual activity or feelings.

GENDERFLUID: This is a person who does not identify themselves as having a fixed gender.

GENDER DYSPHORIA: According to Merriam-Webster[x], gender dysphoria is described as "a distressed state arising from the conflict between a person's gender identity and the sex the person was identified as having at birth." Not every transgender person is diagnosed with Gender Dysphoria. It is characterized by a <u>heightened</u> sense of distress, depression, and/or anxiety directly from the misalignment of gender birth and gender identity.

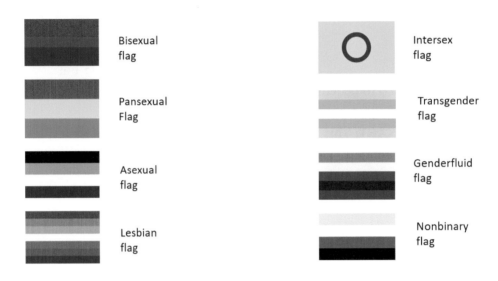

Bisexual flag

Intersex flag

Pansexual Flag

Transgender flag

Asexual flag

Genderfluid flag

Lesbian flag

Nonbinary flag

Ally pride flag

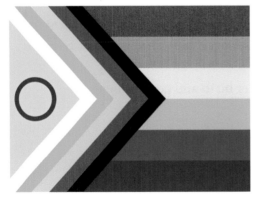

This is the newest pride flag. Each color represents special significance.

Red: Life
Orange: Healing
Yellow: New Ideas
Green: Prosperity
Blue: Serenity
Violet: Spirit
Black/Brown: People of Color
White/Blue/Pink: Trans Community
Yellow w/Purple circle: Intersex People

LGBTQ SYMBOLS

 Gay

Transgender

 Lesbian

Nonbinary

  Bisexual

Heterosexual

Chapter 7

"To shine your brightest light is to be
who you truly are."
~ Roy T. Bennett

As I've walked down this path to educate and enlighten myself about all that is transgender, I've talked with many people who have been kind enough to share their own personal stories with me. I promised I would only use their stories but not their names. These stories were powerful to me as many of them uncovered barriers that make it difficult for them to accept this person's gender identity.

One father shared with me that he could not accept his son's identity because he cannot stand the thought of his son having sex with another man. His son is now a trans woman and as a trans woman, she is straight, meaning she is in a relationship with a man.

Another father told me that his daughter, "claims that she is a man now and she is in a relationship with another woman". He described his thoughts about the situation. He said, "she is doing disgusting things." He said he raised her to be good girl and then she grew up and forgot all of that.

One young man told me that his brother is becoming a woman. He said that he misses his brother because they used to talk about girls all the time together. They would even share personal details about the relationships that each of them had. Now that his brother isn't his brother, he isn't comfortable talking like they once did.

Still another man has a daughter who is transitioning to male. This trans man is interested in men. The father doesn't understand it. He "feels creepy about the whole situation". When I asked him why he feels creepy, he said that his daughter was just fine and then had to go out and be a gay man.

When I spoke with these people, I was not there to judge or try to change their thinking. I just took notes and asked a few questions. I saw a common thread through most of these particular stories. These people were consumed by the sexual part of the picture. They seemed to be missing the point about gender identity and were getting caught up in the sexual orientation component.

These transitioning men and women are following their path to their true identities. The transition is about who they are. Who they love is a very different detail. After hearing this same type of story a number of times, I decided to call some of my friends whose children are grown, just like the age group of these transgender young people whose fathers and brother I wrote about.

Again, I promised confidentiality. I asked the same question to each of these friends whose young adult children are in heterosexual relationships. "Do you ever think about your adult child having sex?" One friend of mine said that as a single mom, she was concerned that her son might not feel prepared for relationships.

He never had a significant male role model. She told him that if he had any questions, she would be happy to talk about whatever he might want advice about. She said he's occasionally asked her advice about buying gifts for his girlfriend but nothing about sex. She said that she does NOT think about him having sex with his girlfriend.

My own experience is this: I have a heterosexual son and a trans daughter. I spend zero seconds every day thinking about my son having sex with anyone. Why would I think about my daughter having sex? They are both consenting adults.

I feel committed to helping not just these people I've written about but everyone to see their adult children as the genders that they identify. If we can support our children to find themselves, they will finally have the opportunity to be themselves. It is absolutely not about the sex that they might be having. It is about the person they are becoming.

Their transition is about their gender identity. It is about WHO THEY ARE. If you can take sex out of the equation, you see that you have a trans son or trans daughter who is becoming their real selves. There are so many things to celebrate when you think about someone finding themself.

When I got divorced, I remember it was so exciting to discover who I really was. I had gotten lost in my marriage and I didn't even know what my favorite color was. When I began living on my own, I learned that I really liked myself, as compared with who I thought I was when I was married. The level of discovery is so much bigger for a person transitioning to another gender.

I hope that you can begin to see your child as the person they were supposed to be all along. As your relationship with your child grows deeper because you are seeing their most authentic self, your respect will grow and your interests stay grounded in their personhood. Most people you know have or have had sex but I imagine you don't think about that part of them. Give your child the strength to become themselves and the freedom to experience life and love in the way they, as respectful adults, so choose.

Chapter 8

"The best gift you are ever going to give
someone – the permission to feel safe in
their own skin, to feel worthy, and to feel
like they are enough."
~ Unknown

Do you see the importance of supporting the transgender person in your life? Here are just some of the ways that you can show your support[xi,xii,xiii,xiv]:

1. Understand that when someone comes out to you, they have decided to open up to you because they love you, respect you, care about you and trust you. Coming out is terrifying. They don't know if you will accept or reject them. Thank them for trusting you. Be aware that this coming out story is theirs to tell.

2. Allow them to make their way around to others if and when they feel ready.

3. Research! Learn about LGBTQ by reading others' stories. Some great books to read:

    a. I Am Jazz by Jazz Jennings and Jessica Herthel

    b. If I Was Your Girl by Meredith Russo

    c. I Wish You All the Best by Mason Deaver

    d. Sorted by Jackson Bird

    e. Cemetery Boys by Aiden Thomas

4. Learn about the organizations that can help support you as you begin this journey with them.

    a. GLAAD.org

    b. TheTrevorProject.org

    c. Trevorspace.org

    d. Gaycenter.org

    e. Cdc.gov/lgbthealth

    f. Hrc.com

    g. Freedomforallamericans.org/

    h. LoveHasNoLabels.com/learn/sexual-orientation

    i.   TransLifeLine.org

    j.   StandWithTrans.org

5. Sign up for a workshop or support group to learn more about being supportive and to find the support that you may want as well.

6. Remember that the person you have loved is still within them. There are definitely some changes happening but it's still them. A huge support is to tell them that you love them. It might not seem like a big deal to you but it's a really big deal to the person who just made themselves vulnerable to tell you something they've been working through to get to this point.

7. Ask questions. "What pronouns would you like for me to use?" "How would you like for me to best support you?"

8. Don't make assumptions or pry into their transgender journey. Not every transgender person transitions medically or even legally. Don't ask questions about their bodies. If that's something that they want to talk about, let them bring it up. Along with that, don't ask about surgeries or hormone therapy.

9. Be respectful and know that they may not know or be ready or willing to share every single detail, especially as they are beginning this personal journey.

10. Listen. Simply listen when they want to talk about the thoughts in their heads. Not everything needs input. As an ally, we are to support and listen but not try to fix everything ourselves.

11. When you hear someone make a crude or demeaning joke or comment on the topic of LGBTQ, stop those hurtful comments.

12. If you see media stories that discriminate against the LGBTQ community, contact GLAAD.org

13. Promote diversity and inclusion. Support LGBTQ organizations and events in your area.

14. When you make a mistake on someone's name or pronouns, simply apologize. Don't think that they didn't hear or notice.

15. Include your own pronouns on email signatures, name badges, and on social media.

16. Show support by wearing a Pride pin or a Pride Ally pin.

17. When you notice a gender-neutral bathroom in a business, thank the management!

18. Follow social media accounts regarding LGBTQ. Like and share their posts.

19. One important fact to remember is that although this person may be transitioning and making life changes, there is SO MUCH MORE to them as individuals. They are people with lots of other facets. Remember to recognize those parts of them and not be completely focused on their gender identity, gender expression or sexual orientation.

20. Think of "Ally" as a verb. Be willing to act on your belief in equity and inclusion.

Chapter 9

"At the end of the day, the goals are simple:
safety and security."
~ *Jodi Rell*

There are certain risks for those in the transgender community. Most of these can be mitigated by allies who are ever-so-slowly changing the narrative for this at-risk group.

- Barriers to healthcare

  - There are situations that cause trans people to seek healthcare in substandard circumstances. If a person feels that they may be harassed or even denied service because they are transgender, they might find unauthorized providers willing to do surgeries or prescribe medications that are unapproved or illegally obtained.

  - Unsafe needle injection practices due to economic factors.[xv]

  - Another barrier is that many providers are not knowledgeable enough about healthcare for the transgender community that they cannot find the resources needed.

- Transphobia violence/hate crimes

  o Transphobia is characterized as negative attitudes, fear, hatred or aversion to social gender expectations. Hate crimes happen when transphobic individuals feel the need to physically punish or humiliate people that defy those notions, leading to discrimination and violence, sometimes leading to murder.

- Discrimination forcing trans people into unemployment or to work in risky occupations

  o When a transgender person is harassed in their job, sometimes they feel unempowered to do their job or do not have the support to be able to complete their job satisfactorily. In the study by UCLA School of Law Williams Institute in April 2021, 45% of employees report hearing anti-LGBTQ remarks.[xvi] Some feel forced to leave for their mental health or even sometimes they are terminated, stemming from the issues related to direct, indirect or subtle discrimination. There are situations where an unemployed transgender person cannot find work so they are forced to work in survival sex work. Studies show that currently black transgender women are at highest risk in this area specifically.[xvii]

- Discrimination by law enforcement

  o In a study by UCLA School of Law Williams Institute in April 2021, 49% of LGBTQ respondents felt that they were treated worse than non-LGBTQ people by law enforcement.[xviii]

- Discrimination at school

  o LGBTQ people surveyed - 57% felt they were treated worse at school than non-LGBTQ people. [xix]

- Discrimination to deny housing, work benefits, or imposing extra burdens that are not imposed on others[xx]

- Rejection of family[xxi]

- Suicide

Chapter 10

"Diversity is the one true thing we all have in common...Celebrate it every day."
~ Winston Churchill

I leave you with these special days for the LGBTQ community and some specific to transgender. You can help them commemorate or celebrate the dates below every year:

- March 31 – International Trans Day of Visibility[xxii]

  o This annual event is to celebrate transgender people and raise awareness about the discrimination they face worldwide. It is also a day to celebrate the trans people who have made contributions to society.

- May 17 – International Day Against Homophobia, Transphobia, and Bi-Phobia[xxiii]

  o This day is observed every year to raise awareness of LGBTQ rights violations and to encourage more interest in LGBTQ rights work worldwide. May 17 was chosen because that was the day in 1990 that the

World Health Organization decided to declassify homosexuality as a mental disorder.

- August 26 – Wear It Purple Day[xxiv]

    o This is an annual event for supporters of LGBTQ to wear purple and celebrate diversity. It was created in response to the suicide of a teen in New Jersey. Purple is a color that represents bringing people from all different backgrounds and creating unity and a more positive perspective of celebrating LGBTQ youth and pride. Wear It Purple Day is a way for allies to show the LGBTQ community that they are seen, heard, loved and that this is a safe space for them.

- October 11 – National Coming Out Day[xxv]

    o October 11, 1987 is the anniversary of the National March on Washington for Lesbian and Gay Rights. This is day is celebrated every year for those who choose to come out positively and help refute the fears and stereotypes of LGBTQ.

- October 19 – International Pronouns Day[xxvi]

    o This day celebrates the use of pronouns, which have become a subject of interest in society overall. Using the set of pronouns that someone asks for you to use for them is a way of validating and affirming that they are equals and deserve the respect and dignity that you would give anyone else.

- First Sunday in November – Transgender Parent Day[xxvii]

    o Mother's Day can be a painful reminder of the desertion for those whose mothers rejected them because of their gender identity. Trans Parent Day is an opportunity to acknowledge the phenomenal parents who love their trans children and support this journey.

- Nov 13-19 – Transgender Awareness Week[xxviii]

    o This is the week leading up to Transgender Day of Remembrance. This week is for raising awareness of the transgender community through education and advocacy activities.

- November 20 – Transgender Day of Remembrance[xxix]

    o On this day, we memorialize those who are no longer alive as a result of Transphobia. This day was founded to draw attention to the continued violence endured by transgender people. This day is and has been honored worldwide since it was founded in 1999.

References

i   https://www.americanprogress.org/article/state-lgbtq-community-2020/

ii   https://williamsinstitute.law.ucla.edu/visualization/lgbt-stats/?topic=LGBT#density

iii   https://williamsinstitute.law.ucla.edu/publications/trans-adults-united-states/

iv   https://www.thetrevorproject.org/research-briefs/trauma-and-suicide-risk-among-lgbtq-youth-july-2022/

v   https://www.learningforjustice.org/magazine/dispelling-six-myths-about-transgender-identity?gclid=CjwKCAjw-L-ZB hB4EiwA76YzObOfcqg3a30nRSLANhMDbgfgkyOSB3l_ X7Fge3g6wmNIACqxmlVRPBoCxZ8QAvD_BwE

vi   https://www.accreditedschoolsonline.org/resources/coming-out-of-the-closet/

vii   Grenny, J., Patterson, K., McMillan, R., Switzler, A., & Gregory, E. (2021). *Crucial Conversations: Tools for Talking When Stakes are High, Third Edition* (3rd ed.). McGraw Hill.

viii   https://pflag.org/hotlines#:~:text=Trans%20Lifeline%3A%20 (877)%20565,need%20to%20survive%20and%20thrive

ix   https://www.glaad.org/reference/terms?response_ type=embed&gclid=CjwKCAjw-L- ZBhB4EiwA76YzObX91oG0OJ8OZ-g99AzwvU8wCb_ EXdEsXJatJ3yGWPZ0Mo1q1UqbSxoCTC0QAvD_BwE

x   ttps://www.merriam-webster.com/dictionary/gender%20
dysphoria#:~:text=Definition%20of%20gender%20
dysphoria,condition%20marked%20by%20such%20distress

xi   https://www.lambdalegal.org/know-your-rights/article/youth-ally

xii   https://www.glaad.org/resources/ally/2?gclid=CjwKCAjw-L-
ZBhB4EiwA76YzOUu2zDkBfIPUy1JF20gIbLSxFyghdVQUeI
1Xq97y0u4oN4egtP93AxoCYVsQAvD_BwE

xiii   https://transequality.org/issues/resources/
supporting-the-transgender-people-in-your-life-a-
guide-to-being-a-good-ally?gclid=CjwKCAjw-L-
ZBhB4EiwA76YzOXasWjfVI-mI1uODerzCxKE-
Rbc0UJ8vSFSf3JtZhTyuvMs5BpjiaRoCWUkQAvD_BwE

xiv   https://www.hrc.org/resources/being-an-lgbtq-ally

xv   https://www.liebertpub.com/doi/10.1089/trgh.2019.0053

xvi   https://www.arcusfoundation.org/wp-content/
uploads/2021/07/US-Employees-Perceptions-of-Anti-
LGBTQ-Discrimination.pdf

xvii   https://www.hrc.org/resources/fatal-violence-against-the-
transgender-and-gender-non-conforming-community-
in-2021

xviii   https://www.arcusfoundation.org/wp-content/
uploads/2021/07/US-Employees-Perceptions-of-Anti-
LGBTQ-Discrimination.pdf

xix   https://www.arcusfoundation.org/wp-content/
uploads/2021/07/US-Employees-Perceptions-of-Anti-
LGBTQ-Discrimination.pdf

xx   https://www.ohrc.on.ca/en/book/export/
     html/11194#:~:text=7.1%20Direct%2C%20indirect%20
     and%20subtle%20discrimination&text=It%20can%20
     happen%20when%20individuals,others%2C%20without%20a-
     %20legitimate%20reason

xxi https://www.ncbi.nlm.nih.gov/pmc/articles/PMC2840628/

xxii https://en.wikipedia.org/wiki/International_Transgender_
     Day_of_Visibility

xxiii https://www.glaad.org/tags/international-day-against-
      homophobia-and-transphobia?gclid=CjwKCAjw-L-ZBh
      B4EiwA76YzOS6TatX2S2pISNkM9ODOrrKtigjMMV-
      fbzYkNkupPONeXhmdk67X_BoCJSwQAvD_BwE

xxiv https://en.wikipedia.org/wiki/Wear_it_Purple_Day

xxv   ttps://www.hrc.org/resources/national-coming-out-day

xxvi https://pronounsday.org/

xxvii https://www.myresourcecenter.org/transgender-parent-
      day/#:~:text=We%20celebrate%20Trans%2DParent%20
      day,than%20how%20they%20were%20raised.

xxviii https://www.theequalityinstitute.com/trans-awareness-
       week?gclid=CjwKCAjw-L-ZBhB4EiwA76YzOQCLPhZI_
       x9LoiaMtHZRYR2m5dgV-gzKQQcJug3XU0eftyawDt3APho
       CwQYQAvD_BwE

xxix https://en.wikipedia.org/wiki/Transgender_Day_of_
      Remembrance#:~:text=The%20Transgender%20Day%20
      of%20Remembrance,as%20a%20result%20of%20transphobia.

AMPLIFLUENCE

AMPLIFY YOUR INFLUENCE

You're the Expert, but are you struggling to Monetize your Authority?

Amplify Your Influence in 3 Sessions

**Speak
Your Message**

**Publish
Your Message**

**Convert
Your Message**

Authors and Speakers often find themselves struggling to build a strategy that actually makes them money.

Check Out All Of Our 'Live' Tour Stops

amplifluence.com

SCAN FOR
TOUR INFO

More Books From

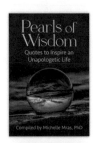

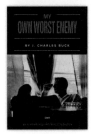

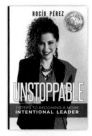
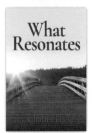

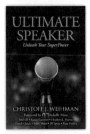

www.PerfectPublishing.com

More Books From  PERFECT PUBLISHING

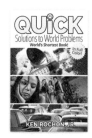

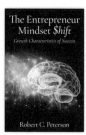
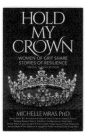

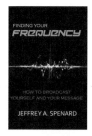

www.PerfectPublishing.com